T0067113

A Homeowner's Guide to the Custom Home Building Process

CHRISTY ANN KICKLIGHTER

BALBOA.
PRESS

A DIVISION OF HAY HOUSE

Balboa Press books may be ordered through booksellers or by contacting:

Balboa Press
A Division of Hay House
1663 Liberty Drive
Bloomington, IN 47403
www.balboapress.com
1 (877) 407-4847

Because of the dynamic nature of the Internet, any web addresses or links contained in this book may have changed since publication and may no longer be valid. The views expressed in this work are solely those of the author and do not necessarily reflect the views of the publisher, and the publisher hereby disclaims any responsibility for them.

The author of this book does not dispense medical advice or prescribe the use of any technique as a form of treatment for physical, emotional, or medical problems without the advice of a physician, either directly or indirectly. The intent of the author is only to offer information of a general nature to help you in your quest for emotional and spiritual well-being. In the event you use any of the information in this book for yourself, which is your constitutional right, the author and the publisher assume no responsibility for your actions.

Any people depicted in stock imagery provided by Thinkstock are models, and such images are being used for illustrative purposes only.
Certain stock imagery © Thinkstock.

Print information available on the last page.

ISBN: 978-1-5043-2800-5 (sc)
ISBN: 978-1-5043-2801-2 (e)

Balboa Press rev. date: 03/23/2015

CONTENTS

Introduction vii

Selecting your Contractor ix

The Cost Estimating Phase

Chapter 1   Bidding & Estimating 3

Chapter 2   Bid Proposal and Clarifications 6

Chapter 3   Options and Value Engineering 14

The Construction Phase

Chapter 4   Contract / Form of Agreement 19

Chapter 5   Insurance and Bonding 21

Chapter 6   Lien Law 24

Chapter 7   Building Permitting 28

Chapter 8   Payment Applications 30

Chapter 9   Change Orders 35

Chapter 10   Project Schedule and Photographs 37

Chapter 11   Material Selections and Submittals 39

Chapter 12   Project Meetings 42

Chapter 13   Quality Control and Punch Lists 44

Post Construction Phase

Chapter 14   Moving In 51

Chapter 15   Warranty and Operation & Maintenance Manual ... 53

Chapter 16   Home Maintenance 55

Construction Glossary 59

About the Author 63

INTRODUCTION

Building your next home should be a pleasure, not a stress-filled cluster of to-do lists, tedious decisions, and "I can't believe that you spent so much money on those granite tops!" Think about it - you've gotten to place where you can actually build a home, from scratch, just the way you've always wanted it - cool right? Yet, so many people get to this point, with all of the positive energy that got them here and get bogged down in fears and worries, and thus the whole experience turns into a nightmare. I have even known couples who have split after building or remodeling home, haven't you?

But it doesn't have to be like that. With just a little bit of information, you can dilute your fears and worries and make this an enjoyable experience. Do not go into it thinking that every contractor wants to rip you off. Do not go into it believing that you're building a money pit. Think of it like buying a new car - you know you have overpaid in the past, you might believe that all car salespeople are crooks, and you have no idea how a car is put together or how to fix one. But that doesn't make it any less fun to drive that new car home with that fresh new car smell. So arm yourself with some knowledge, stay positive throughout the process and really enjoy picturing yourself living in that new home. You don't need to know exactly how to build a home down to the last nail, and you don't have to question every move your contractor makes, but you should be comfortable with your contractor and the information they present to you. As I'll discuss in the next section, selecting your contractor will be the most important decision you make in this whole process. You need to have a high level of trust with them. Your home, or homes, may be your biggest asset, so don't leave it to "Hey, I know this guy whose brother-in-law has a contractor's license and he can really cut you a deal..."

In this book, I'll give you some tips on how to select your contractor and I will layout the basic steps involved in the custom home-building process. It doesn't matter if your home will cost $100,000 or $10,000,000. The differences are only relative to your lifestyle anyway, so it's just a matter of more or less paperwork, permitting, material selections and so on. So relax, start flipping through those pretty home magazines, and enjoy the process.

SELECTING YOUR CONTRACTOR

As I stated earlier, this will probably be the most important decision you make in building your next home. I could also write a book just on selecting your architect or plans. But this book is focused on the construction process, so you should have your architect or plans in place by this point.

(Note: If you are building a model home or have selected a plan from a palette of developer's choices, the construction process is basically the same, but a lot of the leg work will already have been done for you. This is a route you should consider if you don't have the time or desire to really get involved in the details of the floor plan or material selections.)

To begin looking for a contractor, start like you are looking for an auto mechanic or a babysitter, ask your friends and acquaintances. Can they recommend someone that they trust? Is there a local Builder's Association where you can find reputable companies? Ride through neighborhoods that you like and find out who built those homes. Feel free to look on line, but do your homework as well. Many companies may be better at on line marketing than actual building construction. If you commissioned a custom design from an architect's office, they can refer you to local builders that are appropriate for your specific type of construction. If you are building in a development, they will have a list of approved builders for you to choose from.

Next, compile a list of 3-5 companies that you feel can do the job. At this point you may need to have in mind your contract delivery method. That sounds technical, but really it's not. What it means is, how are you going to bid and contract this project? Are you going to hard bid the project to get the lowest bid or are you going to build at a cost-plus basis, with or without a Guaranteed Maximum Price? This is good to have in mind when you are discussing options with each contractor.

Now, interview each company. And remember, your intuition (or gut feeling) is just as good a decision maker as anything else on this list. You will know after a brief interview if you are comfortable and compatible with this builder or not.

Here is a list of questions to ask:

- They should be properly licensed and insured to do the work in your locality, have them show you this. You can even check with the local Building Department or your State's Regulatory Agency yourself to be sure.
- What other projects of similar nature have they completed in your area?
- What are their significant practices, or what makes their homes special or unique?
- Who will be the Project Manager and Superintendent, what are their qualifications?
- What are their contract delivery methods, or will they bid per your instructions? A good contractor should be able to comply with any contract option you choose, although they may have a preferred Form of Agreement.
- Do they require a deposit to start work?

☞ Note: a solid, reputable company should not require a deposit just to begin work or to provide an estimate. They may require a deposit to secure specific, costly materials with a long-lead time, such as custom impact windows/doors, a specific flooring material, etc. - if this is the case, they will provide you with an actual invoice from the vendor

- What is their invoicing or draw schedule? once a month, every other week?
- Can they start your Project right away or is there a wait time?

- What do they anticipate as the total construction time?
- How long will the estimating process take?
- How long will the permitting process take?
- What is their warranty program?
- Do they seem willing to help me with the process or keep me in the dark?
- Ask yourself again, do I trust this person/company. Am I comfortable with them? Will this be an enjoyable experience or a combative one?

Feel free to add to this list or ask anything you deem important. I want to reiterate a point here, since this is important - no solid, reputable company should require a huge deposit just to begin the work without a backup invoice for materials. Let's say they ask for a 20% deposit to begin work on a $1 million Project. That's $200,000 for doing what? This should be a giant red flag that they do not have the cash to comfortably fund your Project in between draws, **or worse**, that they have lost credit capability with their vendors and have to pay cash up front for materials. This scenario also puts them in the position of making their profit on the Project before they even begin, giving you a lot less leverage during the whole process.

After you have interviewed each company, it is time to decide how many of them you would like to bid the Project and how you are going to bid the Project. Remove any Contractors from your list that you would not want to ultimately work with. Remember, depending on the size of the house, construction could take up to a year or more, so that is quite a commitment.

How you bid the job is a matter of personal preference. The two primary bid methods are Stipulated Sum (hard bid) and Cost Plus a Fee (with or without a Guaranteed Max). If your plans are complete and you want to compare prices, you may select 3 to 5 Contractors, or more if you like, and have them give you a hard bid. You are not required to select the lowest bid, but let the bidders be aware of that fact. Why do I say that? I have seen bids come in that are ridiculously lower than the 2nd, 3rd, 4th bids. That should sound an alarm in your head. What did they leave out, what would be the quality of the work, why is their bid so much different than the others? But if the lowest bid or the second lowest bid is comfortable, and you are satisfied with the terms of the Proposal, move on to the contract phase and get to work.

The other method of bidding is Cost Plus a Fee, with or without a Guaranteed Maximum Price. This method can be approached two different ways:

(1) If you have selected the Company that you want to work with and trust that their pricing has historically been in line with other similar Companies, you can start your negotiations and have them propose a Cost Plus Fee estimate.

(2) The other way to approach this would be to have a short-listed group of contractors each give you their General Conditions and Fee Estimate. These are the "soft" costs, or costs to do the work that don't actually end up in your home. General Conditions costs are items like Supervision, dumpsters, permitting, administration and so on.(A more complete list is included in the Estimating Chapter of this book).

In this scenario you could select the contractor with the lowest General Conditions and Fee Estimate and then have them give you a Proposal for the entire project.

Both bid methods - Hard Bid or Cost Plus Fee - are customarily acceptable in the contracting world, it is just a matter of personal preference, and your comfort level with the Bidders. We will discuss estimating and bidding more in that section. So at this juncture, if you have selected your Contractor, you will move onto the estimating and contract phase. If you have a short-list of Contractors, have them provide bids, then make your selection and move onto the contract phase.

THE COST ESTIMATING PHASE

CHAPTER 1

Bidding & Estimating

As discussed earlier, the two primary methods of construction bidding are Hard Bid/Competitive Bid (Stipulated Sum contract method) and Negotiated (Cost plus Fee contract method). With the Competitive Bid process, your group of potential contractors will each give you a Proposed Cost for the Work, based on the plans. They should all be bidding the same set of plans, preferably 90-100% complete, the same specifications, and the same instructions from you and your design team. That way you can compare the bids as apples to apples, meaning the proposals are substantially the same, and you are essentially just comparing prices.

With the negotiated process, you would have previously selected one or maybe two contractors. You would then have them provide a Proposal for the work and you negotiate from there. With high-end custom homes, most bid items are negotiable, but generally you are evaluating the "soft costs". "Soft Costs" are the bid items that are required to do the work, but do not end up in your home, such as Supervision, Markup & Fees, and General Conditions costs. For instance, if you are negotiating with one or two contractors and they propose to do the work for Cost plus a 20% fee, but your golf buddy just got similar work done for Cost plus 16%, you may try to haggle that item. Another reason to use the Negotiated bid method would be that your floor plans and ideas for the home are not 100% complete, and therefore, the pricing phase will need to go through several iterations. With this scenario, I recommend that you have already selected your preferred contractor, so that you can foster a relationship with them and get comfortable with their pricing methods and fees.

The Bidding phase should take from two to four weeks and each bidder should provide a written Proposal and Clarifications, so that you know exactly what is included and what is excluded. The Proposed Cost is a composite of General Conditions costs, Fees, Subcontractors, labor and materials, and historical data. The Bid Proposal is discussed in the next chapter.

Pros and Cons of Competitive Bid vs. Negotiated

Competitive Bidding - PROS	Competitive Bidding - CONS
• Bidders are competing against each other to get to the lowest price • Your plans are 90-100% complete and you can begin the contract phase as soon as the bids are in • Your contract amount will be based on the Hard Bid amount, so you are confident with the price you will end up paying for the construction (unless there are changes)	• The lowest bidder is not always the best bidder or the best fit for you • Offers more opportunity for Change Orders during the Construction phase because the bidder offered you a Hard Bid based on the plans and specifications at bid time • Contractor is less willing to absorb some changes/increases in cost, since they already offered you their lowest price

Negotiated Bidding - PROS	Negotiated Bidding - CONS
• You are choosing up front who you prefer to work with • There is a more open relationship between you and your contractor • You have more input in the pricing phase and ability to negotiate nearly all the phases of the work • Many minor changes can be absorbed into the contract price (thru contingencies & negotiating with Subcontractors) without adding cost to your contract	• Bidders may not be as competitive • The final cost for construction is more open-ended, depending on your input and changes during construction

CHAPTER 2

Bid Proposal and Clarifications

Shown here is a Sample Proposal, followed by a description of each of the components.

 Custom Builders, Inc.
Beach Town, FL   CGC 0001001

SAMPLE PROPOSAL
(Cover Letter)
May 1, 2012

Mr. and Mrs. Homeowner
1234 Second Street
Beach Town, FL 32960

Dear Mr. and Mrs. Homeowner:

Thank you for the opportunity to provide this proposal for your custom home in Vero Beach, FL. The price is based on drawings and specifications as prepared by ABC Architects, dated 1/01/2012; a site review; and the Bid Qualifications attached.

COST FOR CONSTRUCTION $ 1,350,000.00

Thank you and please feel free to call if you have any questions.

Sincerely,

Bob A. Builder
President

Sample Proposal
Page 2

BID QUALIFICATIONS

A. Bid Clarifications:
   1. Bid Price is per plans and specifications listed in the Proposal, with the Qualifications, Exclusions and Allowances listed here.
   2. General Conditions costs are based on a job duration of 12 months.
   3. Full time supervision is included.
   4. Building permit fee is included
   5. Traffic and utility impact fees are included. Fee for a 5/8" water meter is included.
   6. Jobsite cleanup, dumpster fees, and final "construction cleaning" of house are included. Specific deep cleaning per Owner's instruction is not included.
   7. Allowances are included for items not yet specified. When items are selected and priced, a Change Order will be issued to add or deduct from the allowance amount.
   8. Termite treatment, under the slab, is included, and will be provided by XYZ Pest Control, who included a (bond or insurance) on the work.
   9. Fireplaces to be true masonry with brick inside the firebox.
   10. Aluminum railings to have a powder-coat finish.
   11. Structure is bid to withstand 140mph windload.
   12. Roof to be sheathed with 5/8" CDX plywood and 30# felt.
   13. All ceilings to receive ceiling stripping prior to drywall installation.
   14. Manual pull-down attic access ladder is included.
   15. Interior doors bid as pre-hung 1-3/4" LDF (low density fiberboard) doors.

16. All shower enclosures are bid as frameless.
17. French doors : Name-brand, impact resistant, white alum. clad exterior, primed wood interior, multi-point hardware plated in oil-rubbed bronze.
18. Windows: Name-brand, impact resistant, white aluminum, white Seacoast hardware, colonial configuration.
19. Door hardware is bid as Name-brand levers, oil rubbed bronze finish.
20. Association - approved mailbox is included.
21. Wonderboard is included at wet areas of baths.
22. Marble & stone specification - Cast stone a hardscape and porches patterned per landscape designer's drawing; 24"x24" Saturnia flooring at entire first floor, laid square, 18"x18" Saturnia shower walls and floors; slab Saturnia on tub deck.
23. Wood floors are bid as 3" job-finished red oak.
24. Painting price is based on using one color each for walls, trim and ceilings. Color changes and specialty finishes may be extra.

Sample Proposal
Page 3

25. Painting price includes elastomeric paint on exterior and 3-coat system on wood and interior walls.
26. Stucco on exterior walls is 5/8" true cement-based plaster stucco with a smooth finish.
27. Whole house, central vacuum system is included.
28. Pool and spa are included per bid and specifications provided by pool Subcontractor.
29. We have included water piping and electrical conduit to the dock. No electrical wiring or plumbing fixtures are included at dock. Dock is by Owner.

B. Items not included in bid:
1. Architectural and Engineering fees
2. Landscape design and Interior design fees
3. Builders Risk and windstorm insurance
4. Dewatering of site, if required
5. Landscaping and irrigation
6. Dock or dune crossover
7. Site furnishings or decorative pieces
8. Fencing
9. Interior wood shutters and window treatments
10. Gutters and downspouts
11. Screen doors at French doors
12. Anti-fracture underlayment at stone floors, see options
13. Sealer at stone floors, see options
14. Carpeting
15. Wallcovering and specialty finishes
16. Underground trash cans
17. Safe
18. Fountain and decorative fountain pieces

19. Aluminum hurricane panels at un-shuttered openings
20. Pool & spa heater and controls, see options
21. Initial fill of pool and gas tank
22. Gas logs at fireplaces
23. Water treatment system, see options
24. Lightning protection, see options
25. Landscape lighting
26. Stereo/AV system and televisions
27. Lighting controls and home integrations systems
28. Phone/intercom system
29. Generator

Sample Proposal
Page 4

C. Allowances included in bid:
  1. Closet shelving, installed $ 5,000
  2. Custom millwork cabinets, installed $35,000
  3. Stone countertops, installed $21,000
  4. Bath accessories, material only (installed by GC) $ 1,200
  5. Appliances, hoods, and BBQ, installed $17,000
  6. Kitchen, Bath, Bar & Laundry cabinets, installed $75,000
  7. Plumbing fixtures, material only (installed by GC) $15,000
  8. Decorative light fixtures, material only (installed by GC) $ 5,000

D. Options (not currently included in bid):
  1. Pool & spa heater, 400K BTU gas $ 2,105
  2. Jandy RS pool, spa & fountain controller $ 5,725
  3. R.O. water treatment system, per location $ 1,520
  4. Lightning protection system $ 12,525
  5. Anti-fracture underlayment at stone floors $ 5,100
  6. Sealer at stone floors $ 1,950
  7. Remote control gas log set $ 989/each

End of Proposal

The Bid Proposal or Quotation shown here is an example. Each Contractor may have their own format but you should be looking for these basic elements:

- **Cover letter or Proposal letter and Cost** - This is the Cover Letter and should briefly describe what is included in the cost and the documents used to arrive at that cost, such as "plans prepared by ABC Architects".

- **Bid Clarifications** - This is a more detailed listing of items that are included in that cost. This is where you want to look for items such as permit fees, impact fees, supervision costs, and specifications of materials like windows and doors. Sometimes this list may be a complete specification package or the Contractor may refer to Specifications as prepared by your designer.

- **Items Not Include in Bid or Exclusions** - This list will tell you what is NOT included in the Proposed Cost. These are items that YOU will be paying for outside of this Contract or by Change Order. Make sure you are comfortable with these exclusions or you may ask how much it would cost to add any of the items.

- **Allowances** - These are items that the Contractor has included by an allowed dollar amount. This means the item has not been specified and priced out yet. Allowance items are usually finish items that you may not have completely decided on yet, such as carpeting, cabinetry and appliances. In the example above, there is an Allowance for stone countertops of $21,000. When, during construction, you select your stone for the countertops and the Subcontractor prices them at $23,425, the Contractor will issue and Change Order for the difference plus any fees.

Stone Countertop Allowance	-$21,000.00
Stone Countertop Selection	+$23,425.00
Overage	+$ 2,425.00
Contractor's Fee 10%	+ 242.50
Total Change Order	+ $ 2,667.50

- **Options** - This is a list of items that are not included as of now, but you may add them if you like. Discuss with your contractor if you need to decide on any of these items before construction or sometime later in the process.

Once you have reviewed the Proposal, feel free to make a list of any other questions you may have. Maybe there is an item not listed and you are unsure if it is included, or perhaps there are items you would like to remove to save cost. An ethical Contractor will discuss any options with you openly and provide additive or deductive costs until you are satisfied. Just like any other Contract, get comfortable with all the terms before you proceed.

CHAPTER 3

Options and Value Engineering

If after reviewing the initial Proposal, you or your designer still have concerns or want more options, this is when you should consider asking for Options or Value Engineering.

Options - Options means simply that: you request Optional pricing to either add or deduct specific items to the Bid. Maybe you would like to add a fountain or theater system; maybe you decide you want a smaller pool, so that you can spend that money on something else. This is the time to get optional pricing - before you start construction. Typically in construction, the longer you take to decide, the higher the additive price. If you decide to add a masonry fireplace after the masonry shell is constructed, you will not only be paying for the fireplace but the demolition and reconstruction required to install the fireplace. If you wait until the last second to select granite for countertops, it may be back-ordered or only available from a limited source and you'll pay a premium to get it. Material selections should be discussed early in the process, and I have included more on that in Chapter 11.

Value Engineering - Value Engineering (or VE) may sound really technical, but it is simple to understand. If you or your architect/ designer feel that the Proposed Cost is above an expected range, even after you have competitively bid or negotiated the cost, you or your designer may request Value Engineering. In some cases the Contractor may offer this up anyway. This gives the Contractor the opportunity to re-evaluate the entire design of the Project, looking for cost-saving ideas. Your Contractor will draw upon his/her experience in construction and the expertise from Subcontractors and tradesmen to discover cost-saving ideas. Here we are looking to change some aspect of the design that will reduce cost, but without changing the overall intent of the design. For instance: The concrete roofing tile specified in the design documents is imported, rare and very pricy. But after review, the roofing contractor finds an American-made alternative tile that looks similar but is not the exact same color as the one specified. The Contractor can offer you the price reduction with color change, and your original design is still intact. It is always a good idea to ask for input from those who have experience.

THE CONSTRUCTION PHASE

CHAPTER 4

Contract / Form of Agreement

Each Architect and Contractor will have a standard or preferred Contract (or Form of Agreement) that they use, or you may have one you have used before, but they all fall into these basic categories:

- Stipulated Sum
- Cost Plus a Fee, with or without a Guaranteed Maximum Price
- Design - Build

Stipulated Sum - This is a Form of Agreement between Owner and Contractor that states a specific dollar amount to be paid for the specified work. Usually this form is used after you have competitively bid the Project or have agreed to a final price with your selected Contractor. With this form there is no wiggle room for change. If you make a change during the construction process, a Change Order will be issued to add to or deduct from the Contract amount.

Cost Plus a Fee - This is a Form of Agreement between Owner and Contractor that states you will pay the Contractor for the actual cost of the work plus an agreed upon fee. With this agreement, the Contractor will bill you a total of all the actual cost of the work, plus the fee. The periodic Payment Applications will include copies of all invoices for general conditions costs, materials, equipment, labor, and subcontract costs.

With a "Guaranteed Maximum Price" Agreement, the Contractor has estimated the total cost of the work and added a Contingency amount for changes. The "Guaranteed Maximum

Price" cannot be exceeded without a Change Order signed by the Owner.

If the Form of Agreement is "Without a Guaranteed Maximum Price", you are paying actual costs plus fee, as construction proceeds. Although you don't have the security of knowing the total final actual cost, the Contractor will have provided you with an estimate so you have an idea of the final cost. And you are only paying for actual invoices submitted plus fee. This option is typically used when the design is not 100% complete at the Estimating phase, so costs will still need to be determined as the construction progresses.

Design - Build - This is a form of Agreement between the Owner and Contractor/Designer. In this scenario, your designer/architect and contractor are the same entity or are contractually connected. Therefore, you are paying for all of the design, specification and construction work to one entity - the Design-Build group. A Design-Build contract is applicable for fast-tracked construction or production homes. The Construction can begin as soon as plans are complete enough to obtain Building Permits. And as design progresses, specifications and costs will be updated. This is usually also a Cost Plus scenario, since the full design is not complete at the start of the work.

In residential construction, many standardized Forms of Agreement used by Architects and Contractors are issued and approved by the AIA (American Institute of Architects) and the AGC (Associated General Contractors of America). Go to AIA.org or AGC.org for more information and a complete listing of contract documents.

CHAPTER 5

Insurance and Bonding

Hopefully by this stage, you are aware that your Designer and Contractor should be properly licensed and insured. Ask them for proof and contact your local building department or regulating agencies for proof as well. The local building department maintains records of the licensing and insurance for all contractors approved to do work in that city or county. A contractor cannot pull a permit or request inspections without being properly licensed and insured.

Also, almost every state has a regulatory agency with a website where you can check on the licensing status of any company. In Florida, for example, go to www.myflorida.com and click on "Licensee Search". There you will find if a Contractor's license is active, inactive, expired, or revoked, and if any complaints have ever been filed.

In regards to insurance, there is more than one type of insurance involved in construction and you should familiarize yourself with the basics.

- **General Liability** - Liability insurance protects the insured (the Contractor) from the risks of liabilities imposed by lawsuits and similar claims. It protects the insured in the event he or she is sued for claims that come within the coverage of the insurance policy.
- **Errors and Omissions (Professional Liability)** - This is carried by your Design professional or your Contractor if you have a Design Build contract. If a Design flaw or error causes a financial loss or issue with the construction, it should be covered by this policy.

- **Builder's Risk** - In Residential construction, this can be covered by your homeowner's policy or by the Contractor. Check your Contract to confirm if it is included or not included. If the Contractor includes it, it will be treated as another cost to you, so you should check with your personal Homeowner's policy as well, to compare prices. Builder's Risk covers damage to buildings while they are under construction. Builder's risk covers perils such as fire, wind, theft and vandalism and many more. It typically does not cover perils such as earthquake, flood or wind in beach zones unless the policy has been specifically endorsed to do so.

- **Automobile** - This covers the Contractor's vehicles and automotive personal liability during work times.

- **Worker's Compensation** - This is a statutory, mandated insurance program that <u>ALL</u> licensed contractors are required to carry. It provides wage replacement and medical benefits to employees (the construction workers) in the case of workplace accidents. Each state has a Division of Worker's Compensation web page where you can verify that an employer has a current active policy.

 A NOTE ABOUT WORKER'S COMP INSURANCE - If your contractor offers you a "Worker's Comp Exemption Certificate" be aware of this - the Exemption is only for the individual who owns the company and no one else. If the contractor has employees who perform work and hires subcontractors who perform work, they ALL must be covered by a Worker's Comp Policy!

- **Performance and Payment Bond** - Bonds are typically not used in residential construction, but can be added if you feel you need the extra security. A Performance and Payment Bond is a surety bond issued by an insurance company to guarantee satisfactory completion of a project by a contractor.

If the Contractor defaults during construction, the bonding company will hire another Contractor to complete the project and insure that bona fide subcontractors get paid as well. Bonds are generally issued for governmental, municipal, educational and large commercial construction. Homeowners are somewhat protected from Contractor default by state lien laws which are discussed in the next chapter.

As with any contract, have your legal counsel or insurance agent review it to make sure that your bases are covered.

CHAPTER 6

Lien Law

Lien laws or Mechanic's lien laws are state statutes that attempt to protect workers, subcontractors and homeowners from Contractor default. Each state regulates their own lien laws, so consult with your attorney or lender about the laws in your state.

Lien laws provide for certain subcontractors and workers on a construction project to lien the property that was improved if they did not receive payment from the Contractor. As a homeowner, you will want to at least be aware of the documents involved, so that you don't get freaked out when you see them, thinking that your Contractor just ran away to the islands with your latest payment.

- **Notice of Commencement** - a legal form that is signed by the property Owner granting permission to begin the work. This form is usually required to be notarized and recorded in a court of law, and can be issued by your attorney, lender or building department.
- **Notice to Owner** - a legal notice that is filed by subcontractors, sub-subcontractors, suppliers or laborers on a construction project. Any subcontractor, sub-subcontractor, supplier or laborer must file this document according to legal guidelines in order to maintain lien rights, in the case of non-payment. The Owner, lender, Contractor, or any other party of interest named in the Notice of Commencement will be copied when a Notice to Owner is properly filed and recorded.
- **Partial Release of Lien** - As the project moves along progress payments will be made by the Contractor to the Subcontractors, sub-subcontractors, suppliers and laborers.

With each payment the Contractor should have the payee sign a Partial Release of Lien and provide copies to you with the next Payment Application. This provides evidence that the Contractor is paying his vendors with the money you are giving him.

- **Final Release of Lien** - This form is signed by the payee when the Contractor issues a final contract payment. Before you issue a final contractual payment to the Contractor, make sure to get Final Releases from all entities that have filed a Notice to Owner, as this forfeits their lien rights. You may also request Final Releases from any subcontractors that performed work on the property (not just the ones who filed a Notice to Owner), just for peace of mind. Any ethical Contractor will have no problem providing releases because they will have paid all their bills in a timely fashion.

- **Contractor Final Affidavit of Payment** - This is a statutory notarized form, signed by the Contractor which states that "All work to be performed under the contract has been fully completed, and all lienors under the direct contract have been paid in full." This form is required and gives the owner some assurance that payments issued to the Contractor have been appropriately allocated to the subcontractors and laborers who have performed work on the project.

 Notice of Non-Payment - This is the form you do NOT want to see. You or your lender will receive a Notice of Non-Payment if a lienor has not been paid and their account is seriously past due, usually 90 days or more. This form is a prerequisite to filing a formal lien on the property, which means the lienor will be looking to file a lien if payment is not made. Contact your Contractor immediately to get this issue resolved.

NOTICE OF COMMENCEMENT

PERMIT #_____**TAX FOLIO #**_____

State of _____, County of _____, the undersigned hereby gives notice that improvement will be made to certain real property, and in accordance with state statute #xxx.xx, the following information is provided in this Notice of Commencement.

1. LEGAL DESCRIPTION OF PROPERTY (AND STREET ADDRESS IF AVAILABLE):
_____

2. GENERAL DESCRIPTION OF IMPROVEMENT:
_____

3. OWNER INFORMATION OR LESSEE INFORMATION (If lessee contracted for the improvement)
    a. Name:_____
       Address:_____
    b. Interest in property:_____
    c. Name and address of fee simple title holder (if other than owner):
_____

4. CONTRACTOR:
    Name:_____
    Address:_____
    Phone number:_____

5. SURETY COMPANY (If applicable, attach a copy of the payment bond):
    Name:_____
    Address:_____
    Phone number:_____

6. LENDER/MORTGAGE COMPANY:
    Name:_____
    Address:_____
    Phone number:_____

7. PERSONS WITHIN THE STATE OF _____ DESIGNATED BY OWNER UPON WHOM NOTICES OR OTHER DOCUMENTS MAY BE SERVED:
    Name:_____
    Address:_____
    Phone number:_____

8. IN ADDITION TO HIMSELF OR HERSELF,
    a. Owner designates_____of _____to receive a copy of the lienor's notice.
    b. Phone number:_____

9. EXPIRATION DATE OF NOTICE OF COMMENCEMENT:_____
    (The expiration date is one year from the date of recording unless a different date is specified)

WARNING TO OWNER: ANY PAYMENTS MADE BY THE OWNER AFTER THE EXPIRATION OF THE NOTICE OF COMMENCEMENT ARE CONSIDERED IMPROPER PAYMENTS UNDER STATE STATUTE #XXX.XX AND CAN RESULT IN YOUR PAYING TWICE FOR IMPROVEMENTS TO YOUR PROPERTY. A NOTICE OF COMMENCEMENT MUST BE RECORDED AND POSTED ON THE JOB SITE BEFORE THE FIRST INSPECTION. IF YOU INTEND TO OBTAIN FINANCING, CONSULT WITH YOUR LENDER OR AN ATTORNEY BEFORE COMMENCING WORK OR RECORDING YOUR NOTICE OF COMMENCEMENT.

UNDER PENALTIES OF PERJURY, I DECLARE THAT I HAVE READ THE FOREGOING AND THAT THE FACTS IN IT ARE TRUE TO THE BEST OF MY KNOWLEDGE AND BELIEF.

_____
SIGNATURE & TITLE OF OWNER or LESSEE or OWNER'S AUTHORIZED AGENT

THE FOREGOING INSTRUMENT WAS ACKNOWLEDGED BEFORE ME THIS ____DAY OF_____,20____,BY:

_____
AS_____FOR_____
(name of person type of authority)   (name of party on behalf of whom instrument was executed)

____Personally known or ____produced identification - type of identification produced_____

_____
NOTARY SIGNATURE   PRINTED NAME   NOTARY SEAL

Sample Notice of Commencement

Lien laws are enforced by States so the forms and requirements in each state will be slightly different. To learn more about lien laws in different states, you may consult your lender or attorney or perform a web search. For example, to research lien laws in a specific state, simply search "lien laws in Florida" or "mechanic's lien law in New York".

The mere fact that lien laws exist tells us that enough contractors have defaulted or misallocated funds so as to warrant enacting a law. This is certainly a shame and one of the reasons that construction contractors have such a bad reputation. As I stated earlier - the most important decision you will make in building your home is selecting the Contractor. You want to be able to trust them with your home and your money.

CHAPTER 7

Building Permitting

Building permits are issued by municipalities - the city or county where the property exists.

☞ Only properly licensed contractors may apply for building permits. In some instances homeowners can apply for their own permits, but unless you have experience with the process, save yourself the hassle and let the Contractor do the dirty work. Permitting is something contractors deal with all the time and they know the tricks to getting it done. And they will be the first to tell you, like dealing with any government agency, it can be quite aggravating. All you should be required to do is sign the permit application and Notice of Commencement. If permit fees were included under the scope of your contract, you will pay for the cost through your scheduled contract invoices. If permit fees were not included in your contract, the Contractor will invoice you separately for the direct costs, with receipts from the building departments.

Permits are issued by the building department and will also involve different city or county departments and fees - such as traffic impact fees, utility departments, utility connection fees, fire departments, health departments and so on. During the permitting process, building officials are reviewing the plans for code compliance to ensure the health and safety of the public. Construction cannot begin until a permit is issued and the permit process for single family homes generally takes four to six weeks. The permitting process may take longer if you are in a heavily populated area or less time if you are in a remote area where there are fewer permits being issued.

Once a permit is issued, construction can begin. The building department will then perform scheduled inspections of the construction at certain milestones. This is to ensure that the construction is actually progressing according to the approved, permitted plans. Again, this is your contractor's burden to carry since they are the license holder. Any issues of non-conformance discovered by the building inspector will be red-flagged. This means that the next phase of construction cannot begin until the issue is resolved and re-inspected. The Contractor and/or Designer will address any issues to the approval of the building department as soon as possible. They don't want construction to be held up either.

Upon or near completion of the project, the contractor will call for a final inspection. After approval of the final inspection, the building department will issue a Certificate of Occupancy. The Certificate of Occupancy states that the building is fit for use by the public. Be sure to get a copy of this document, as it will be requested by lenders, utility departments, and any other entity with an interest in the property.

CHAPTER 8

Payment Applications

Now, the not-so-fun part, is having to pay for all this goodness. During the contract phase, you should have agreed to some form of payment schedule. Generally speaking, however, most builders invoice once per month or according to a scheduled set of milestones. Some may ask for deposits early on to order specific materials. Any deposits requested prior to work being performed should be backed up by actual invoices for actual materials ordered, like expensive flooring or windows. The builder may also invoice early in the process for mobilization costs. Mobilization costs include permitting, insurance, set-up costs for trailers and equipment, and any other preparatory work.

If your project is funded by a lender, they may have their own payment schedule, dependent on milestone inspections. In either case, whether monthly or by milestone, payment is expected within 10-30 days after approval of the invoice - check your contract. It really is in your best interest to keep the cash flowing regularly (as long as you have no construction issues) since this will keep the workers coming back your project every day and not leaving for greener pastures.

Some contracts may include a provision for retainage. Retainage is a percentage withheld from the payment amount, usually 5-10%. The percentage amount is withheld from every invoice, until the end of the project. So that at project completion, you have a tidy hold-back as incentive to get all work finished to your satisfaction.

I probably do not need to tell you this, but review every payment application thoroughly. You need to make sure that all items invoiced are actually completed, in place or on order in the case of material deposits. If a lender is funding the project, they may have their own inspectors to approve invoices as you go along. Or if you have a contract administration agreement with your architect/designer, they will inspect the project for you and sign-off on the invoices. Several professional associations publish payment application forms that are accepted by lenders and architects, or your builder may have a form of their own. In essence, however, all payment applications should show the following:

- The name & address of the Project, Owner, and Contractor and invoice date
- A summary page with total contract amount, total current invoice amount, total of any change orders and total of any retainage, if applicable
- A detailed listing of construction items, invoiced by percentage of completion (for stipulated sum contracts) or actual amount of completion (for cost plus fee contracts)
- An area for the contractor to sign and an area for the lender or architect to approve and sign, if applicable
- Some forms may require the Owner's signature as well
- Some forms may require notarization

Here is a basic sample payment application for residential construction, based upon our sample Proposal:

APPLICATION FOR PAYMENT: Number 3 for August 2012

To Owner: Mr. & Mrs. Homeowner   Project: Custom Residence,

From Contractor: Custom Builders,   Via Architect: ABC Inc.
                Beach Town, FL   Architects

1.	Original Contract Price	$1,350,000.00	
2.	Net Change by Change Orders	3. $ 12,500.00	Certified true and correct:
4.	Current Contract Price	$1,362,500.00	Contractor: Custom Builders, Inc.
5.	Total Work to Date	$ 339,800.00	By: *Bob A. Builder,* President
6.	Retainage Amount (xx%)	N/A	Date: August 25, 2012
7.	Total Work less Retainage	$ 339,800.00	
8.	Less Previous Payments	$ 167,450.00	Architect: ABC Architects
9.	**Amount Due this Application**	**$ 172,350.00**	By: *Arnold Architect,* Principal
10.	Balance to Finish	$1,022,700.00	Date: August 27, 2012

APPLICATION FOR PAYMENT #3 - BACKUP SHEET

DESCRIPTION	SCHEDULED VALUE	PREVIOUS	THIS PERIOD	BALANCE
1. General Conditions	$ 170,857	$ 17,700	$ 14,000	$139,157
2. Sitework	$ 21,200	$ 21,200	$ 0	$0
3. Concrete & Masonry shell	$ 186,500	$110,609	$ 72,600	$ 3,291
4. Hardscape	$ 25,000	$0	$0	$ 25,000
5. Alum. gates & railings	$ 11,600	$0	$0	$ 11,600
6. Carpentry Lumber	$ 56,000	$0	$ 13,184	$ 42,816
7. Carpentry Labor	$ 74,000	$0	$ 14,000	$ 60,000
8. Wood Trusses	$ 15,600	$0	$ 15,600	$0
9. Closet Shelving Allowance	$ 5,000	$0	$0	$ 5,000
10. Millwork Cabinets Allowance	$ 35,000	$0	$0	$ 35,000
11. Kitchen, Bath Cabinets Allow.	$ 75,000	$0	$0	$ 75,000
12. Insulation	$ 4,800	$0	$0	$ 4,800
13. Roofing	$ 57,800	$0	$ 18,000	$ 39,800
14. Windows, Doors, Hdwr	$ 72,600	$0	$0	$ 72,600
15. Mirrors & Showers	$ 4,000	$0	$0	$ 4,000
16. Stucco	$ 39,500	$0	$0	$ 39,500
17. Drywall & Plaster	$ 28,400	$0	$0	$ 28,400

18. Stone & Tile Flooring	$ 69,500	$0	$0	$ 69,500
19. Stone Countertops Allow.	$ 21,000	$0	$0	$ 21,000
20. Hardwood Flooring	$ 14,500	$0	$0	$ 14,500
21. Painting	$ 54,000	$0	$0	$ 54,000
22. Bath Accessories Allow.	$ 1,200	$0	$0	$ 1,200
23. Appliances Allowance	$ 18,000	$0	$0	$ 18,000
24. Swimming Pool & Spa	$ 26,500	$0	$0	$ 26,500
25. Plumbing	$ 19,900	$0	$ 4,000	$ 15,900
26. Plumbing Fixtures Allow.	$ 15,000	$0	$0	$ 15,000
27. HVAC System	$ 22,400	$0	$0	$ 22,400
28. Electrical	$ 39,700	$0	$ 2,500	$ 37,200
29. Light Fixtures Allowance	$ 5,000	$0	$0	$ 5,000
30. Special order items	$ 10,900	$0	$0	$ 10,900
31. Vacuum & Security Systems	$ 4,900	$0	$0	$ 4,900
32. Contractor's Fee 12%	$ 144,643	$ 17,941	$ 18,466	$ 108,236
33. Change Order #1	$ 9,000	$0	$0	$ 9,000
34. Change Order #2	$ 3,500	$0	$0	$ 3,500
TOTALS	$1,362,500	$167,450	$172,350	$1,022,700

CHAPTER 9

Change Orders

Change orders have gotten a nasty reputation in the construction business, evoking thoughts of the "old bait and switch". But actually, change orders are simply additions or deductions from the original Agreement price based on changes made to the scope of work. As long as you are familiar with the terms of your Agreement and what is included and excluded in the price, you need not fear the change order. In fact, many a contractor would rather not deal with them at all, since changes in the scope can cause scheduling delays, the need to re-do work or re-order materials, or confusion on the work site. But they are a fact of life in construction and your Agreement should spell out the protocol and fees for executing a change order, so that you are not blindsided by the process.

A change order can be initiated by several factors. You, as the homeowner, may decide to change a color, material selection or dimensions of a certain room. An architect, interior designer or landscape architect may make changes at your request to some design feature. Or perhaps you decide to change the den into a full in-home theater. Other changes may arise from the field, due to some unforeseen circumstance. In any event, refer to the terms in your Agreement before signing a change order. You should also be somewhat comfortable with the price, so negotiate or double-check the pricing if there is opportunity to do so. Technically, a change order cannot be executed on site until you have approved it and signed it. A Contractor should not surprise you with a change order that they say was necessary for construction without your prior knowledge.

CHANGE ORDER

Contractor: Custom Builders, Inc.   Change Order #: 1
          Beach Town, FL   Date: July 4, 2012

Project: Custom Home for   Description: Change roof tile selection
          Mr. & Mrs. Homeowner

The Contract is changed as follows:

1. Original roof tile selection, white concrete square tile	$	(20,000)
2. New roof tile selection, variegated clay Spanish S tile	$	25,000
3. Additional nails & labor for new required nailing pattern	$	3,000
4. Project Management change fee	$	75
5. Subtotal	$	8,075
6. Contractor's fee 12%	$	969
TOTAL CHANGE ORDER	**$**	**9,044**

Original Contract Amount was	$ 1,350,000
Net change by previous Change Orders	$ 0
Contract Amount prior to this Change Order	$ 1,350,000
Contract will be increased (decreased) by the Change Order	$ 9,044
New Contract Amount, including this Change Order	$ 1,359,044

CONTRACTOR   **OWNER**   **ARCHITECT**
Custom Builders, Inc.   Mr. & Mrs. Homeowner   ABC Architects

_____   _____   _____
Signed   Date   Signed   Date   Signed   Date

CHAPTER 10

Project Schedule and Photographs

Before construction begins, your contractor will prepare a schedule of work to be performed, step by step. A schedule is used to anticipate the ordering of materials and scheduling of labor, and to keep track of the job's progress. The schedule is usually in the form of a bar graph and there are many computer applications available to create and track construction scheduling. A schedule lists the construction tasks, start dates and completion dates of each task, and shows how each task relates to the next. Schedules can then be updated weekly, monthly or by milestones. The project schedule should be included with job progress meetings or payment applications.

Another way to keep track of a job's progress is with photos, either aerial or ground level. If your contractor includes this service, they will share the photos with you on paper, electronically or on a website. The internet is full of applications now that allow you to log-on to your project privately to view the progress. Photographic documentation is also quite helpful should you ever have a construction issue or claim for latent defect. So I recommend that you take your own pictures or hire it out if this service is not included in your contract.

CHAPTER 11

Material Selections and Submittals

Now I don't know about you, but making material selections is one of my favorite parts of the whole construction process. This is when you get to magically turn the visualization of your dream home into reality. You get to actually see and feel the pieces and parts that will make up that dream home. And material selections are made at many different stages of construction, which helps to make the whole construction process much more enjoyable.

Before the construction machine even turned on, you visualized your home in the form of a floor plan. Then, either with the help of a designer or by selecting a pre-designed plan, you put that visualization into motion and the construction wheels began to turn. Next you thought about the look of your house - stucco or siding? one story or more? what type of roof? and so on. And now at different points along the way, you get to shop for appliances, cabinets, flooring, and fixtures. How cool is that?

But even if you are not as excited about this as I am, not to worry. Your contractor and/or designer will help you along with a material selection schedule to keep you on track. They may also make suggestions, offer assistance, have pre-selected palettes from which to choose, or send you to their preferred vendors. And if you have hired an Interior Designer, they will do most of the leg work for you. Interior Designers will bring you material samples and escort you to the various material supply facilities. Remember, also, that if you are building in a community, many of the selections will be made for you by the community association.

Submittals are the vehicle by which you approve the materials that you have selected. As you make selections, the contractor and/

or designer will provide a submittal for your approval. A submittal is a physical piece of the item (like a floor tile) or paper documentation with a color chart (like an appliance specification) that you sign off on. Your signature or approval gives the contractor the go ahead to order that item. Be aware that if you are ordering custom materials, once you sign off, you are buying them. If you discover after the fact that you really don't like the color of the granite countertops, but you had approved the submittal, you probably will have to pay for the granite chosen as well as a the cost of a new selection.

Shown here is a standard material selection list, listed by priority. For instance, windows, doors and roofing need to be selected during the planning stage as they need to be incorporated into the drawings. Paint colors and landscaping can be selected toward the end of the project. A larger, more complicated home, will have a longer list of selections, but this list covers the main priorities.

CUSTOM RESIDENCE
OWNER SELECTIONS BY PRIORITY
(Deadlines will be provided for each item)

1. Windows and exterior doors
2. Roofing material
3. Type of water treatment system
4. Plumbing fixtures and trim
5. Interior trim and doors
6. Cabinetry and casework
7. Appliances, in conjunction with cabinetry
8. Electrical walk-thru - locations of switches and outlets
9. Security, TV, Stereo/AV, vacuum, and phone system with locations
10. Countertops
11. Ceramic tile and stone flooring
12. Wood flooring
13. Closet components
14. Paint colors, interior and exterior
15. Door hardware
16. Color for metal/wood shutters and railings
17. Decorative light fixtures
18. Pool waterline tile and pool finish
19. Landscape lighting
20. Landscaping
21. Mirrors, shower doors, bath accessories and other decorative items

CHAPTER 12

Project Meetings

The frequency and duration of project meetings again will depend on the complexity of the project. In general terms, however, project meetings should be held at least once a month. The homeowner (or representative), contractor (or representative) and contractor's field superintendent should definitely be present. If your architect is involved in construction administration, they will also want to attend. If you have a designer or decorator, they will need to attend when design decisions need to be made. I also find it of great assistance for pertinent subcontractors to attend as well, and I highly recommend it. Since the subcontractors' personnel will be the actual persons assembling the project, it is to everyone's benefit that they get the opportunity to offer suggestions and know your concerns. It is also helpful for the subcontractors to know exactly what the homeowner, architect and/or designers are aiming for in the finished product.

At a minimum, project meetings should cover -
- Current project status
- Current schedule and any delays
- Material selections as needed
- Any concerns about material deliveries or lack of labor force
- Current invoice to Owner for work completed
- Meetings can be held in an office or on site if you need to review physical areas of concern

Areas that you should review physically on site might include:
- Cabinetry and appliance locations
- Windows and doors
- Electrical/data/phone/AV outlets
- Hardscape and landscaping
- Paint colors

Even though meetings are held to discuss project status and details, never hesitate to contact your contractor or architect directly if you have a question or concern. They should be available to assist you at any time during working hours, and sometimes even after hours, depending on your relationship. Also know that if you are not physically located near the project, perhaps out of the state or country, use technology as your eyes and ears. Have your contractor or architect provide you with progress reports with photos/videos by email or by logging onto a website.

Go into each meeting or site visit with a positive attitude. You want a beautiful home and the contractor wants to provide a product to be proud of. If you have a valid concern, attempt to withhold judgment and blame until you get the whole story. Problems can get solved more smoothly if all parties are working toward the same end goal, rather than each trying to prove the other wrong.

CHAPTER 13

Quality Control and Punch Lists

Although the concept of quality is relative to the scope of the project, much like cost or complexity, product quality should be taken seriously by your builder. Most reputable builders will have a Quality Control Program documented and enforced in the field. This Program may include checklists, inspection reports, means & methods of installation, and computer software applications designed to manage the job flow. There should also be a chain of command instituted for the application of quality control in the field.

something like this:
Contractor > Contractor's Project Manager > Contractor's Superintendent > Site Foremen > Subcontractor's Foreman > Tradespeople/installers

If your architect or designer is providing construction administration duties, they will also perform job site inspections, usually monthly, and notify the contractor of any defects or issues.

The simplest and one of the most effective methods of monitoring quality control is through the use of Daily Logs and photographs. The Contractor's Superintendent or Foreman should be in charge of this task. Daily Logs are daily reports that document what happened on site that day - what workers were there, what items were constructed and installed, any issues that arose, and even how the weather affected the work. As the homeowner, you do not need to review or approve this documentation, but it is helpful for you to be aware of it. So should a problem arise, where a portion of the project did not turn out quite as expected, the contractor can follow the paper trail to find out what happened and how it can be rectified.

DAILY LOG

PROJECT: _Smith Residence_   DATE: _March 17, 2011_

WEATHER: AM _Partly cloudy, 75 deg._   PM _Rain, 80 deg._

SCOPE OF WORK:	CREW SIZE:
Site work:	
Laborers: _day labor_	2
Concrete/Masons: _form slab, stage rebar_	4
Steel:	
Carpenters:	
Roofers:	
Insulators:	
Glazers:	
Drywall:	
Stucco:	
Acoustic:	
Tile/Flooring:	
Painters:	
Plumbing/Fire Sprinkler: _under-slab piping_	2
HVAC:	
Electricians:	
Additional Notes:	
Problems/Delays: _afternoon rain, form crew left at 2:30_	
Material Delivered & Rental Equipment:	
Owner/Architect Changes:	

SUPERINTENDENT SIGNATURE: _____Bob A. Builder_____

45

The Punch List - this is one portion of Quality Control where you as homeowner should definitely be involved. If you cannot physically do this yourself, you will need to arrange for a representative or consultant to do so. About a month prior to the scheduled final completion date, you or your representative will walk through the job site. You then create a Punch List by walking through the project, thoroughly viewing all the pieces and parts, and making a note of anything that needs to be completed, fixed or changed. If your architect or designer is providing administration services, they will create their own Punch List as well. By this point in the Project, most major issues should have already been resolved and the Punch List should consist of minor details, such as paint touch-up, pieces of cabinetry or door hardware, equipment startup, and such. A sample punch list is shown here.

Custom Builders, Inc.
Vero Beach, FL

MEMORANDUM

Date: 11/17/2004

To: Subcontractors

Reference: Smith Residence **PUNCH LIST**

Subcontractors – please have all items completed by Tuesday, Nov. 23, 2004.

Drywall Contractor
1. Complete ceiling tile
2. Install sound panels

Plumbing
1. Recirculating pump & pipes
2. Connect two burner stove
3. Pour pads at septic
4. Complete hot water startup

Electrical
1. Complete security system work.
2. Demonstrate system
3. Exterior light at garage
4. Seal conduit with foam at panel
5. Missing bulb at exterior fixture
6. Panel schedules
7. Labels
8. Power & switch to recirc. Pump.
9. Final submittals/warranties to office

Air Conditioning
1. Complete thermostats
2. Do test & balance items
3. Clean units
4. New filters
5. Attach all fan units fully
6. Remove misc. items from attic
7. Final submittals/warranties to office

Aluminum fabricator
1. Install missing handrails
2. Install front gate
3. Fix gate at AC enclosures

Flooring
1. Complete vinyl base in Laundry Room
2. Fix tile at mop sink

Windows
1. Complete one window trim at rear elevation

Roofing
1. Submit Owner's warranties to office

Painting
1. Typical all – touch up doors & frames
2. Touch up walls inside and out
3. Fix stucco cracks and touch up.

Superintendent – Install:
1. Shower rods
2. Trimout glass block
3. Install grab bars
4. Remove trailer
5. Sod patch
6. Gravel at two locations
7. Complete door hardware
8. Compile close-out documents/meeting

It is also standard practice to withhold a portion of the final payment owed to the contractor until all punch list items are completed. This gives the contractor a little incentive to wrap up any loose ends. If your contract has a retainage clause, perhaps you are still withholding 5 or 10%. As long as your contract allows it, you may continue to hold back retainage until all work is satisfactorily completed. If you do not have a retainage clause, you may propose to hold back a certain lump sum amount, and this amount should be close to the value of the work left to be completed.

Hopefully at this stage in the process, you have a comfortable open dialogue with your contractor and are able to resolve any issues through honest discussions. As with any contractual process, do not sign any final releases, final affidavits or release final payment until you are satisfied that all contractual obligations have been met.

POST CONSTRUCTION PHASE

CHAPTER 14

Moving In

Time to move in! Let's all do a happy dance! Pat yourself on the back for making it to this stage of the process. You envisioned your dream home, you put the process in motion, you made every minor and major decision along the way, and now you can enjoy what you and your team have created. If you have moved into a new home before, you know there are still a few more hoops to jump through and maybe more aggravation ahead, but don't get frustrated. Just make your checklist and get going. If you are new to the area you are moving to, ask your contractor for contact information for local utilities, service providers, movers, maintenance companies, lawncare professionals and such. They may even have a checklist already prepared for you.

- Certificate of Occupancy (C.O.) - This is a final certificate of completion issued by the building department that states your home is ready for occupancy. Be sure to get your copy of this. The local utility authorities will request the C.O. before setting up service. Lenders and insurers will also probably ask for a C.O. before finalizing documents or issuing final payment to the contractor.
- Utilities - Get a complete listing of the utility authorities that have jurisdiction where you live. Your contractor should have this as they have had to work with the utilities during the construction process. There will likely be fees required to startup or connect service. Check your contract again to see what fees were included or excluded.
  - ✓ Electric
  - ✓ Water

- ✓ Sewer or septic tank, also involves the local health department
- ✓ Fire department
- ✓ Phone, cable, internet
- ✓ Solid waste, trash, recycling
- ✓ Security monitoring provider, may involve a local police department permit
- ✓ Specific town or community services, if you are in a community development

- Moving in - Although most contractors are not going to help you move in clothes and furniture, they will help with specific requests that require planning. You might have large trees or plants that are being delivered, a piano or pool table or statue that needs to get inside the house before all the doors are installed, or some artwork that gets installed as part of the wall or floor finish. Depending on your contract and relationship, the contractor may not charge you at all for this work or only charge you an hourly rate for the workers to get it done. I recommend that you prepare this list of items well before project completion and discuss it with your contractor. If they can get the work done while they are still there working, any costs will be less than if they have to make special trips for special requests.

CHAPTER 15

Warranty and Operation &
Maintenance Manual

Sometime near final completion, either just before final payment or right after, your contractor should provide to you a Warranty and Maintenance Manual, also referred to as an O&M Manual. If they do not, just ask for one. This Manual is a compilation of the warranties and maintenance manuals from the contractor, the major subcontractors and equipment manufacturers. It may be bound in a three-ring binder or something similar, or submitted to you electronically. Although the technical part of the manual may not interest you, you should browse through it as some warranties may need to be signed by you and mailed back, just like when you purchase a new refrigerator. The warranty period and terms offered by your contractor should be clear and as agreed to in the contract, and the final completion date should be listed. A typical residential Warranty Manual may include the following, give or take:

CUSTOM HOME, BEACH TOWN, FL
OWNER'S WARRANTY & MAINTENANCE MANUAL
TABLE OF CONTENTS

Vendor Name	Description
1. Custom Builders (Contractor)	Warranty Letter
	List of Subcontractors & Suppliers (with phone numbers & addresses)
	Material selections
2. ABC Engineering	Materials testing reports
3. Surveying Company	Surveys
4. XYZ Architects	Final plans and Completed final punch lists
5. Landscape Nursery	Landscaping materials certification & warranty
6. Pest Control Service	Termite Treatment Certificate
7. Insulation Contractor	Insulation Certificate
8. Roofing Contractor	Roofing warranty & inspection schedule
9. Hardware Supplier	Door & hardware warranties
	Door Hardware Schedule
10. Window & Doors	Warranty letter & Notice of Acceptance (NOA)
11. Paint Vendor	Paint color selections
12. Appliance Vendor	Appliance warranties
13. Plumbing Contractor	Warranty & Owner's manual
14. HVAC Contractor	Test & balance report; Warranty & Owner's manual
15. Electrical Contractor	Warranty & Owner's manual
16. Pool Contractor	Warranties & equipment maintenance schedule

CHAPTER 16

Home Maintenance

Well, since our technology has not yet reached the point where homes can maintain themselves, we are going to have to manage that task. Thankfully, however, there are plenty of options available for home maintenance, depending upon your personal and budgetary preferences. As a rule of thumb, you should plan on spending about 1-2% of the cost of your home on annual maintenance and repairs. Therefore, if the total construction cost of the home is $550,000, you could spend $5500-$11,000 on maintenance and repairs per year. Some years you may not spend near that much, but another year you may have to put out a large sum of money to replace a roof, for example. So figure these estimates as an average overall and remember to save or budget for the expense.

- **Do-it-yourselfers** - If you or your friends are handy or in the trades, this is the option for you. You will save the cost of labor by performing the work yourself, even though you will have to buy the materials. Many people who are not construction workers can learn to build their own decks, paint the house, or replace toilets and light fixtures, for instance. But know your own limits. Do not attempt any type of work you are not comfortable with, or you may have to pay someone to fix your mistakes as well as perform the repair.

  If you have friends or family in the trades (ones that are trustworthy enough to barter with), the barter system works great also. Let's say you are a dentist and your brother-in-law is a roofer, for example. You can offer to exchange dental services for the roofing work.

- **Home maintenance insurance/Home warranty plan** - This is a good option if you need to stay in a budget and do not intend to perform the work yourself. A home maintenance or warranty plan is an insurance policy that you purchase, usually on an annual basis, that agrees to provide you with no-cost or discounted repair and replacement services. The costs and benefits vary widely, as with any insurance policy, so you will need to research this on-line or with an agent to find the proper coverage.

- **Home maintenance contractors** - Most high-end residential contractors have a home maintenance division in-house or can refer you to another company that provides home maintenance services. A home maintenance contractor is a service company that will perform the repairs or replacement and charge you on a time-and-material cost basis. You may prefer to sign an annual contract with agreed upon labor charges, pay a lump-sum amount once a year that covers specific items, or pay as you go. Discuss the options with your builder.

- **Or any combination of the above**

IN CLOSING

Now that we have navigated through the basic road map of the construction process, my hope is that you look forward to the journey. Building your new home can and should be an enjoyable experience - by educating yourself, staying positive and visualizing the outcome - your dream house. Select a builder that you trust and that you feel will work with you toward the end goal. Make a list of all your responsibilities as outlined in this guide and break them down into bite-sized chunks. You don't have to do it all in one day, go one step at a time in order of priority. Keep motivated by seeing yourself picking out furniture and living in that house. Meet every challenge with an optimistic attitude and knowledge. And before you know it, it will all come together and you'll be planning a house-warming party.

Congratulations! I hope your new home provides you years of enjoyment and a peaceful retreat from the rest of the busy world.

CONSTRUCTION GLOSSARY

Allowance - an allowed dollar amount included in the contract to be used for unselected products or materials, that will be selected at a later date

Construction Delivery Method - the type of contract agreement between the Owner and Contractor, such as Stipulated Sum (competitive bid), Cost plus a Fee, Design-Build, etc.

C.O. - Certificate of Occupancy, issued by the building department after all final inspections have passed

Draw - an invoice from the contractor to the Owner or lender, i.e. "a monthly draw"

Dry-in - the stage when the building shell has been completed enough to keep out the weather. Generally after the roofing paper or underlayment has been installed and the exterior windows and doors are installed and closed.

Hardscape - the exterior site features, such as pavers, driveways, decks and privacy walls

Hose bibb - an exterior water spigot or faucet

HVAC - Heating, Ventilation and Air Conditioning system

In lieu of (I.L.O.) - instead of; in replacement of ("ABC Contractor offers to provide concrete roofing tiles in lieu of clay barrel tiles for a savings of $xxx dollars.")

Lien Release or Waiver of Lien - A signed and notarized form issued by a subcontractor or supplier releasing its lien and right to claim a lien for labor, services or materials furnished on the property

Mobilization - logistical setup of the project site which includes clearing the property, coordinating with on-site utilities and permitting departments, delivering construction trailers and equipment, installing temporary fencing and barricades, and similar work

Mud - wet concrete, when it's being poured

N.I.C. - Not in Contract, not included

Permit - a form issued by a local building department or utility department that permits you to make improvements to your property

Punch list - a list of minor, uncompleted work items and repairs compiled by the Contractor, Architect and/or homeowner, near the end of the project

Rough-in - the stage of construction when electrical conduits, AC ductwork and plumbing lines are being laid out and installed, and before they are covered up by concrete, wood or drywall

Subcontractor - a trade contractor that works for the general/building contractor under a subcontract to perform a specified portion of the construction

Trade (construction trade) - a specialty profession within the construction industry, i.e. plumbing trade, electrical tradesman, carpentry trade, roofing, etc.

Trim-out - the stage of construction when plumbing fixtures, light fixtures, door & cabinet hardware, etc. is being installed

Truss - an engineered metal or wood fabrication that is installed on top of the walls to form the roof structure. Usually trusses are in the shape of a triangle.

Water closet - commonly called a toilet

ABOUT THE AUTHOR

Christy has a Bachelor of Science in Building Construction from the University of Florida and is currently licensed in the State of Florida as a Certified Building Contractor. She has been working in construction for over twenty-two years and has experience in all phases of construction - estimating, bidding, supervision, project management, job-cost accounting, contract administration, scheduling, permitting and safety.

She built her first personal home at the age of 22. She has managed tens of millions of dollars worth of high-end custom homes and renovations on the East Coast of Florida.

Christy currently resides in Vero Beach, Florida with her husband and children, and manages a local construction company. In her spare time she enjoys all the fun-in-the-sun that Florida has to offer.

Printed in the United States
By Bookmasters